Low-Carb Diet Cookbook for Two

365-Day Perfectly Portioned Recipes for Tasty, Budget-Friendly Low-Carb Meals for Everyday Wellness

Hurlny Tillr

Table of Contents

Introduction

This Low-Carb Diet Cookbook for Two has more than just tasty and wholesome recipes inside. You'll also find invaluable tips for streamlining your kitchen time, reducing food waste, and enhancing your meals with cooking hacks and simple techniques to add even more flavor to your favorite dishes.

Ditch the refined and processed ingredients and reawaken your taste buds to the vibrant flavors of fresh foods that will satisfy your hunger and leave you feeling more energized. The Low-Carb Diet Cookbook for Two makes it easy with 365-Day Perfectly Portioned Recipes for Tasty, Budget-Friendly Low-Carb Meals for Everyday Wellness to make sure you're starting out on the right path. This essential couple's cookbook has more than just tasty and wholesome recipes inside.

The low-carb diet is one of the most popular diets for lasting weight loss and total health. But getting started can feel like an overwhelming lifestyle change—especially if you're doing it alone. Low-Carb Diet for Two is here to help by teaching you how to embrace the low-carb diet with two people in mind.

Chapter 1: Breakfast

Sweet Potato Hash with Bacon, Eggs, and Cheese

Serves: 2

Prep Time: 5 minutes

Cook Time: 20 minutes

Ingredients:

- 4 bacon slices
- 1 jewel or garnet sweet potato or yam, peel and diced
- 1/2 onion, diced
- Kosher salt
- Freshly ground black pepper
- 2 large eggs
- 2 ounces goat cheese

Directions:

1. Heat a medium oven-safe skillet over medium- high heat. Cook the bacon for 3 to 4 minutes per side, until crisp. Transfer to a paper towel-lined plate. Crumble the bacon after it has cooled.
2. Remove all but about 1 tablespoon of the bacon fat from the skillet. Cook the sweet potato and onion in the bacon fat, stirring frequently, for 8 to 10 minutes, until the vegetables are softened and beginning to brown.
3. While the vegetables are cooking, preheat the broiler on high.
4. Stir the bacon into the vegetable mixture, season with salt and pepper, then spread the mixture into an even layer in the skillet. Make four small indentations in the vegetable mixture. Crack an egg into each indentation, and season with salt and pepper. Place the pan under the broiler and cook for 3 to 4 minutes, until the egg whites are set but the yolks are still runny.
5. Remove the skillet from the broiler and immediately crumble the cheese over the top. Serve hot.

Per Serving:

Calories: 472; Total Fat: 31g; Saturated Fat: 14g; Cholesterol: 258mg; Sodium: 1,160mg; Total Carbohydrates: 17g; Sugars: 5g; Protein: 30g

Chorizo and Egg Breakfast Burritos

Serves: 2
Prep Time: 5 minutes
Cook Time: 10 minutes

Ingredients:

- 4 ounces chorizo, loose or removed from its casing
- 2 large eggs
- 2 teaspoons reduced-fat milk
- Pinch kosher salt
- Pinch freshly ground black pepper
- 2 (8-inch) flour tortillas, warmed
- 1/4 cup shredded cheddar cheese

Directions:

1. Heat a medium skillet over medium-high heat. Add the chorizo and cook, stirring and breaking up the meat with a spatula, for about 5 minutes, until browned. Drain the excess fat from the skillet.
2. In a small bowl, whisk together the eggs, milk, salt, and pepper. Add the egg mixture to the skillet with the chorizo and cook, stirring, for about 3 minutes, until the eggs are fully set.
3. Lay the tortillas on a work surface, and spoon half the egg mixture into the center of each tortilla. Sprinkle the cheese over the filling.
4. Fold the sides of each tortilla over the egg filling, then roll up the burrito from the bottom to the top. Serve immediately.

Per Serving:

Calories: 532; Total Fat: 35g; Saturated Fat: 14g; Cholesterol: 251mg; Sodium: 1,229mg; Total Carbohydrates: 26g; Sugars: 2g; Protein: 27g

Breakfast Quesadillas

Serves: 2

Prep Time: 5 minutes

Cook Time: 15 minutes

Ingredients:

- 4 large eggs
- 1 tablespoon reduced-fat milk
- Kosher salt
- Freshly ground black pepper
- 1 tablespoon unsalted butter
- 2 (10-inch) flour tortillas
- 1/2 cup shredded Monterey jack cheese
- Nonstick cooking spray

Directions:

1. In a medium bowl, whisk together the eggs, milk, and salt and pepper to taste.
2. In a medium nonstick skillet, melt the butter over medium-high heat. Add the eggs and cook, stirring frequently, for 2 to 3 minutes, until set. Transfer the eggs to a plate or bowl.
3. Sprinkle half the cheese over one tortilla in an even layer. Top with the cooked eggs, then the remaining cheese. Place the second tortilla on top.
4. Wipe out the skillet you used to cook the eggs, then spray with cooking spray and heat over medium-high heat.
5. Cook the quesadilla in the skillet for 3 to 5 minutes, until golden brown on the bottom. Carefully flip it over and cook until the second side is golden brown and the cheese is melted, about 3 minutes more.
6. Remove the quesadilla from the pan and let it stand for a few minutes before slicing it into eight wedges.
7. Divide the quesadilla wedges between two plates and serve.

Per Serving:

Calories: 518; Total Fat: 30g; Saturated Fat: 13g; Cholesterol: 413mg; Sodium: 897mg; Total Carbohydrates: 3g; Sugars: 3g; Protein: 25g

Tomato, Zucchini, and Cheese Frittata

Serves: 2
Prep Time: 5 minutes
Cook Time: 15 minutes

Ingredients:

- Nonstick cooking spray
- 4 large eggs
- 1/2 teaspoon kosher salt
- 1 zucchini, shredded on the large holes of a box grater
- 1 medium tomato, diced
- 1 tablespoon finely chopped fresh chives
- 1/2 cup shredded cheddar cheese, divided

Directions:

1. Preheat the oven to 400°F.
2. Spray a large oven-safe skillet with cooking spray and heat over medium-high heat.
3. In a medium bowl, whisk together the eggs and salt. Stir in the zucchini, tomato, chives, and 1/4 cup of the cheese. Pour the egg mixture into the skillet, and sprinkle the remaining 1/4 cup cheese on top. Let the mixture cook for 2 to 3 minutes, until the bottom begins to set.
4. Transfer the skillet to the oven and bake for 12 to 14 minutes, until the eggs are set. Remove the skillet from the oven and let rest for 5 minutes before slicing the frittata into wedges to serve. Serve hot, at room temperature, or chilled.

Per Serving:

Calories: 287; Total Fat: 20g; Saturated Fat: 9g; Cholesterol: 402mg; Sodium: 910mg; Total Carbohydrates: 7g; Sugars: 4g; Protein: 21g

Apple Cinnamon Pancakes

Serves: 2

Prep Time: 5 minutes

Cook Time: 5 minutes

Ingredients:

- 2/3 cup buttermilk pancake mix
- 1/2 teaspoon ground cinnamon
- 2/3 cup applesauce
- 1½ tablespoons reduced-fat milk
- Nonstick cooking spray
- Maple syrup, for serving

Directions:

1. In a medium bowl, stir together the pancake mix and cinnamon. Stir in the applesauce and milk. Mix well.
2. Spray a large skillet with cooking spray and ladle the batter into the skillet, using about 1/4 cup batter per pancake. When the pancakes begin to bubble on top and their edges start to firm, flip them and cook for 2 to 3 minutes more, until golden brown on the second side.
3. Serve hot, drizzled with maple syrup.

Per Serving:

Calories: 221; Total Fat: 2g; Saturated Fat: 1g; Cholesterol: 6mg; Sodium: 219mg; Total Carbohydrates: 51g; Sugars: 36g; Protein: 3g

Eggs Benedict

Serves: 2
Prep Time: 15 minutes
Cook Time: 15 minutes

Ingredients:

- 4 slices Canadian bacon
- 2 egg yolks
- 1½ teaspoons freshly squeezed lemon juice
- 1/4 teaspoon kosher salt
- 5 tablespoons unsalted butter, melted
- 4 large eggs
- 2 English muffins, split and toasted
- Freshly ground black pepper

Directions:

1. Place a medium saucepan or deep skillet filled with about 3 inches of water over high heat. This will be your egg-poaching pan.
2. In a large skillet, cook the Canadian bacon over medium-high heat for about 2 minutes per side, until it is sizzling and lightly browned. Remove the skillet from the heat.
3. To make the sauce, in a blender, combine the egg yolks, lemon juice, and salt. Blend on high speed for about 30 seconds, until the mixture lightens to a pale yellow. With the blender running at low speed, drizzle the melted butter into the mixture. Continue blending until the mixture is thick and well combined. If it is too thick, add a small amount of warm water to thin it.
4. When the egg-poaching water is boiling, reduce the heat to low and crack in the eggs carefully. Raise the heat a bit if needed-you want the water to be gently simmering, with some small bubbles around the eggs. Set a timer for 4 minutes.
5. To assemble the eggs Benedict, place a slice of Canadian bacon on top of each toasted English muffin half. Using a slotted spoon, carefully lift the eggs out of the water one at a time, letting the excess water drain. Place an egg on top of each muffin half.
6. Drizzle the sauce over the tops of the eggs, dividing it equally. Garnish with freshly ground pepper, and serve immediately.

Per Serving:

Calories: 702; Total Fat: 49g; Saturated Fat: 25g; Cholesterol: 698mg; Sodium: 1,647mg; Total Carbohydrates: 31g; Sugars: 4g; Protein: 37g

Greek Scramble Breakfast Wraps

Serves: 2

Prep Time: 5 minutes

Cook Time: 5 minutes

Ingredients:

- 4 large eggs
- Kosher salt
- Freshly ground black pepper
- 2 tablespoons olive oil, divided
- 2 cups baby spinach
- 2 (10-inch) whole-wheat tortillas or wraps
- 8 cherry tomatoes, halved
- 1 cup crumbled feta cheese

Directions:

1. In a medium bowl, whisk together the eggs, salt and pepper to taste, and 1 tablespoon water.
2. In a medium nonstick skillet, heat 1 tablespoon of the olive oil over medium-high heat. Add the eggs and cook, stirring frequently, for 2 to 3 minutes, until set. Transfer the eggs to a plate or bowl.
3. Wipe out the skillet, add the remaining 1 tablespoon olive oil, and heat over medium heat. Add the spinach and cook, stirring frequently, for about 2 minutes, just until the spinach wilts. Transfer the spinach to a plate or bowl.
4. Wipe out the skillet again. Over medium-high heat, briefly heat the tortillas, one at a time, for about 30 seconds per side.
5. Lay the warm tortillas flat on a work surface. Add half the eggs, spinach, tomatoes, and cheese down the center of each tortilla.
6. Fold the sides of each tortilla over the egg filling, then roll up the wrap from the bottom to the top. Serve immediately.

Per Serving:

Calories: 650; Total Fat: 42g; Saturated Fat: 15g; Cholesterol: 422mg; Sodium: 1,321mg; Total Carbohydrates: 43g; Sugars: 6g; Protein: 28g

Baked Eggs with Spinach and Goat Cheese

Serves: 2

Prep Time: 5 minutes

Cook Time: 10 minutes

Ingredients:

- Nonstick cooking spray or butter, for preparing the ramekins
- 1/2 cup chopped baby spinach
- 1½ ounces goat cheese
- 2 large eggs
- 2 tablespoons heavy (whipping) cream
- 1 teaspoon chopped fresh herbs (basil, thyme, or oregano)
- Kosher salt
- Freshly ground black pepper
- Toasted whole-wheat or sourdough bread, for serving (optional)

Directions:

1. Preheat the oven to 375°F and spray 2 (6-ounce) ramekins with cooking spray.
2. Add half the spinach to each ramekin, then crumble the cheese on top, dividing it equally.
3. Crack an egg into each ramekin. Pour 1 tablespoon of the cream over each egg. Sprinkle the herbs over the top of each ramekin, and season with salt and pepper.
4. Bake for 8 to 12 minutes, until the egg whites are set but the yolk is still runny, and the cream bubbles around the edges.
5. Remove from the oven and let cool for a couple of minutes before serving.
6. Serve immediately, with toasted whole-wheat or sourdough bread, if desired.

Per Serving:

Calories: 185; Total Fat: 15g; Saturated Fat: 8g; Cholesterol: 216mg; Sodium: 237mg; Total Carbohydrates: 2g; Sugars: 1g; Protein: 1g

Lox and Eggs Sandwiches

Serves: 2

Prep Time: 5 minutes

Cook Time: 5 minutes

Ingredients:

- 2 English muffins, split
- 2 tablespoons salted butter, divided
- 4 large eggs
- Kosher salt
- Freshly ground black pepper
- 2 tablespoons cream cheese
- 2 slices nova lox

Directions:

1. Toast the English muffins, then spread the cut sides with 1 tablespoon of the butter.
2. In a medium bowl, whisk together the eggs and salt and pepper to taste.
3. In a medium nonstick skillet, melt the remaining 1 tablespoon butter over medium-high heat. Add the eggs and cook, stirring frequently, until almost set, about 2 minutes. Fold the cream cheese into the eggs and cook for another minute or so, until the cheese is melted and the eggs are fully cooked. Remove the pan from the heat.
4. Equally divide the egg mixture between two of the English muffin halves. Drape one slice of lox over each, then top with a second English muffin half. Serve immediately.

Per Serving:

Calories: 538; Total Fat: 32g; Saturated Fat: 16g; Cholesterol: 439mg; Sodium: 983mg; Total Carbohydrates: 44g; Sugars: 6g; Protein: 26g

Strawberry and Brie French Toast Sandwiches

Serves: 2

Prep Time: 5 minutes

Cook Time: 5 minutes

Ingredients:

- 2 ounces brie cheese, sliced
- 4 sandwich bread slices
- 1/4 cup strawberry preserves or strawberry jam
- 2 large eggs, beaten
- 2 teaspoons reduced-fat milk
- Nonstick cooking spray

Directions:

1. Divide the Brie slices between two of the slices of bread. Top with the strawberry preserves, then place the remaining bread slices on top.
2. In a wide, shallow bowl, whisk together the eggs and milk.
3. Spray a large nonstick skillet with cooking spray and heat over medium heat.
4. Dunk the sandwiches into the egg mixture, coating both sides well.
5. Cook the sandwiches in the skillet for 2 to 3 minutes per side, until golden brown. Serve hot.

Per Serving:

Calories: 420; Total Fat: 15g; Saturated Fat: 7g; Cholesterol: 215mg; Sodium: 528mg; Total Carbohydrates: 51g; Sugars: 23g; Protein: 20g

Chapter 2: Soups and Sandwiches

Black Bean Soup

Serves: 8

Prep Time: 10 minutes

Cook Time: 20 minutes

Ingredients:

- 1 tablespoon olive oil
- 1/2 onion, diced
- 1 (15-ounce) can black beans, drained and rinsed, divided
- 2 cups vegetable broth
- 1 cup salsa (mild, medium, or hot)
- 2 teaspoons chili powder or store-bought kosher salt (optional)

Directions:

1. In a stockpot or Dutch oven, heat the oil over medium-high heat. Add the onion and cook, stirring frequently, for about 5 minutes, until softened.
2. Add the beans, reserving 1/2 cup, the broth, salsa, and chili powder and bring to a boil. Reduce the heat to medium-low and simmer, stirring occasionally, for 10 minutes. Remove the pot from the heat.
3. Using an immersion blender or a countertop blender (be careful when blending hot soup!), puree the soup until smooth.
4. Return the soup to the heat and stir in the reserved 1/2 cup beans. Cook over medium heat for 5 more minutes, until heated through.
5. Add salt or other seasonings to taste. Serve hot.

Per Serving:

Calories: 323; Total Fat: 10g; Saturated Fat: 2g; Cholesterol: 0mg; Sodium: 927mg; Total Carbohydrates: 44g; Sugars: 6g; Protein: 19g

Creamy Tomato Soup

Serves: 2
Prep Time: 10 minutes
Cook Time: 10 minutes

Ingredients:

- 1 (28-ounce) can whole tomatoes (preferably san marzano)
- 2 tablespoons olive oil
- 1 large garlic clove, minced
- 1 cup vegetable broth
- 3 tablespoons heavy (whipping) cream
- 2 tablespoons chopped fresh basil, divided kosher salt
- Freshly ground black pepper

Directions:

1. In a blender, puree the tomatoes and their juices and set aside.
2. In a stockpot or Dutch oven, heat the oil over medium heat. Add the garlic and cook, stirring, for 30 seconds, until fragrant.
3. Add the pureed tomatoes and broth and bring to a gentle boil. Reduce the heat to medium-low and simmer for 10 minutes.
4. Stir in the cream and 1 tablespoon of the basil. Season with salt and pepper.
5. Serve hot, garnished with the remaining 1 tablespoon basil.

Per Serving:

Calories: 282; Total Fat: 23g; Saturated Fat: 8g; Cholesterol: 33mg; Sodium: 823mg; Total Carbohydrates: 18g; Sugars: 10g; Protein: 5g

Chicken caesar wrap

Serves: 2
Prep Time: 5 minutes
Cook Time:

Ingredients:

- 2 whole-wheat wraps or large whole-wheat flour tortillas
- 1 cup chopped romaine lettuce
- 3/4 cup shredded or diced cooked chicken
- 1/4 cup caesar salad dressing
- 3 tablespoons grated parmesan cheese

Directions:

1. On a clean work surface, lay the wraps out flat.
2. Top each wrap with half the lettuce and half the chicken. Drizzle the dressing and sprinkle the cheese over the filling on of each wrap, dividing evenly.
3. Fold the sides of each wrap over the filling, then roll up the wrap from the bottom to the top like a burrito. Slice each wrap in half and serve immediately.

Per Serving:

Calories: 440; Total Fat: 25g; Saturated Fat: 6g; Cholesterol: 55mg; Sodium: 716mg; Total Carbohydrates: 27g; Sugars: 2g; Protein: 27g

Pumpkin Curry Soup

Serves: 2

Prep Time: 10 minutes

Cook Time: 10 minutes

Ingredients:

- 1 tablespoon olive oil
- 1 tablespoon Thai red curry paste
- 2 cups chicken broth or vegetable broth
- 1 (15-ounce) can pumpkin puree
- 3/4 cup coconut milk
- 2 tablespoons chopped fresh cilantro

Directions:

1. In a stockpot or Dutch oven, heat the oil over medium heat. Add the curry paste and cook, stirring, for 1 minute. Stir in the broth and pumpkin and bring to a boil.
2. Stir in the coconut milk and cook for 3 to 4 minutes, until the soup is very hot.
3. Serve hot, garnished with the cilantro.

Per Serving:

Calories: 364; Total Fat: 43g; Saturated Fat: 19g; Cholesterol: 25mg; Sodium: 542mg; Total Carbohydrates: 21g; Sugars: 7g; Protein: 9g

Bacon and Egg Salad Sandwiches

Serves: 2
Prep Time: 10 minutes
Cook Time: 5 minutes

Ingredients:

- 4 bacon slices
- 4 hard-boiled large eggs, peeled and chopped
- 3 tablespoons mayonnaise
- 1 dill pickle, chopped
- Kosher salt
- Freshly ground black pepper
- 2 croissants, split

Directions:

1. In a large skillet, cook the bacon over medium- high heat until crisp, about 5 minutes. Transfer to a paper towel-lined plate and let cool.
2. In a medium bowl, combine the eggs, mayonnaise, and pickle. Crumble the bacon into the mixture and stir gently to combine. Season to taste with salt and pepper.
3. Spoon the egg salad into the croissants and serve immediately.

Per Serving:

Calories: 759; Total Fat: 55g; Saturated Fat: 18g; Cholesterol: 466mg; Sodium: 1,571mg; Total Carbohydrates: 33g; Sugars: 6g; Protein: 32g

Spicy Butternut Squash Soup

Serves: 2

Prep Time: 10 minutes

Cook Time: 20 minutes

Ingredients:

- 1 tablespoon avocado oil
- 1/2 cup chopped yellow onion
- 2 garlic cloves, minced
- 1½ cups frozen butternut squash cubes
- 1¼ cups reduced-sodium vegetable broth
- 1 (15.5-ounce) can cannellini beans, rinsed and drained
- 1/4 teaspoon kosher salt
- 1/8 teaspoon freshly ground black pepper
- 1/4 teaspoon red pepper flakes
- 2 teaspoons white-wine vinegar

Directions:

1. In a Dutch oven or soup pot, heat the oil over medium heat until it shimmers.
2. Add the onion, and sauté for 3 minutes, until soft. Add the garlic, and sauté, stirring frequently, for another 1 minute, until fragrant.
3. Add the butternut squash, and cook for 3 minutes, until no longer frozen.
4. Add the broth, then stir in the beans. Season with the salt and pepper, and stir to combine. Cover, and bring to a boil. Reduce the heat to medium-low, and simmer for 5 minutes.
5. Stir in the red pepper flakes, and cook for another 3 minutes. Remove from the heat.
6. Carefully transfer to a blender. Place the lid on the blender but remove the plug. Hold a clean kitchen towel over the opening on the lid, leaving a small space for steam to escape. Blend for 1 to 2 minutes, until creamy.
7. Divide the soup evenly between 2 bowls. Drizzle each with 1 teaspoon of vinegar.

Per Serving:

Calories: 403; Fat: 8g; Carbohydrates: 67g; Fiber: 13g; Sugar: 6g; Protein: 19g; Sodium: 1,491mg

Noodle Soup

Serves: 2
Prep Time: 15 minutes
Cook Time: 15 minutes

Ingredients:

- 6 ounces extra-firm tofu
- 3 scallions
- 2 teaspoons cornstarch
- 1 tablespoon avocado oil
- 2 carrots, diced (about 1 cup)
- 1 cup sliced baby portabella or white mushrooms
- 3 cups reduced-sodium vegetable or chicken broth
- 3 ounces dried egg or rice noodles
- 1/4 teaspoon kosher salt (optional)

Directions:

1. Line a plate with a paper towel. Place the tofu on top, cover with another paper towel, and set a heavy plate on top. Drain for 10 minutes.
2. Meanwhile, trim and thinly slice the scallions, keeping the green and white parts separate.
3. Using a sharp knife, cut the tofu into 1/2-inch dice. Transfer to a shallow bowl or plate, and toss with the cornstarch.
4. In a Dutch oven or soup pot, heat the oil over medium heat until it shimmers. Add the tofu, and sear 2 minutes, turning occasionally. Transfer to a plate.
5. To the same pot, add the scallion whites, carrots, and mushrooms. Reduce the heat to medium-low, and cook, stirring frequently, for 3 minutes, until the vegetables have softened slightly.
6. Add the broth, increase the heat to medium-high, and bring to a boil. Add the noodles, and cook according to the package instructions. Taste, and add the salt if desired. Remove from the heat.
7. Divide the tofu evenly between 2 bowls. Ladle the soup over the tofu, and garnish with the scallion greens.

Per Serving:

Calories: 352; Fat: 18g; Carbohydrates: 48g; Fiber: 4g; Sugar: 6g; Protein: 15g; Sodium: 758mg

Spicy, Cheesy Potato Soup

Serves: 2
Prep Time: 10 minutes
Cook Time: 15 minutes

Ingredients:

- 1 tablespoon olive oil
- 1 (15-ounce) package frozen diced potatoes and onions, thawed
- 4 cups low-sodium vegetable broth
- 2 teaspoons Cajun seasoning (I like tony chachere's), plus more if needed
- 1 cup whole milk
- Kosher salt (optional)
- 1 cup shredded sharp cheddar cheese, plus additional for garnish

Directions:

1. In a stockpot or Dutch oven, heat the oil over medium-high heat. Add the potatoes and onions and cook, stirring, until heated through.
2. Add the broth and Cajun seasoning and bring to a boil. Reduce the heat to medium-low, cover, and let the soup simmer for about 10 minutes, until the potatoes and onions are very tender. Stir in the milk and remove from the heat.
3. Using an immersion blender or countertop blender (be careful when blending hot soup!), puree the soup until smooth and thick. Add salt or more Cajun seasoning to taste. Reheat the soup over medium heat just until heated through.
4. Stir in the cheese until it melts and is incorporated.
5. Serve hot, with extra cheese sprinkled on top.

Per Serving:

Calories: 556; Total Fat: 30g; Saturated Fat: 15g; Cholesterol: 72mg; Sodium: 603mg; Total Carbohydrates: 46g; Sugars: g; Protein: 26g

Taco Chicken Soup

Serves: 2
Prep Time: 5 minutes
Cook Time: 15 minutes

Ingredients:

- 2 cups chicken broth
- 1½ cups refried beans
- 1½ cups canned fire-roasted diced tomatoes with green chile
- 1 cup shredded cooked chicken
- 1 tablespoon chili powder or store-bought kosher salt
- Freshly ground black pepper

Directions:

1. In a stockpot or Dutch oven, combine the broth, beans, tomatoes and their juices, chicken, and chil powder and bring to a boil over medium-high heat.
2. Reduce the heat to low, cover, and simmer for 15 minutes.
3. Season with salt and pepper. Serve hot.

Per Serving:

Calories: 349; Total Fat: 20g; Saturated Fat: 2g; Cholesterol: 94mg; Sodium: 1,042mg; Total Carbohydrates: 35g; Sugars: 3g; Protein: 37g

Chicken Salsa Verde Soup

Serves: 2

Prep Time: 5 minutes

Cook Time: 20 minutes

Ingredients:

- 1 tablespoon avocado oil
- 1 (8- to 10 -ounce) boneless, skinless chicken breast
- Kosher salt
- Freshly ground black pepper
- 1 (14.5-ounce) can fire-roasted tomatoes, juices drained by half
- 1 cup store-bought salsa verde
- 1 (14.5-ounce) can black beans, rinsed and drained

Directions:

1. In a small Dutch oven or stockpot, heat the oil over medium-high heat until it shimmers.
2. Season the chicken on both sides with salt and pepper. Add to the pot, and sear for 4 to 5 minutes on each side, until no longer pink inside. Transfer to a cutting board.
3. Reduce the heat to medium. In the same pot, combine the tomatoes with juice, salsa verde, and beans. Stir to combine. Cook, stirring occasionally, for 5 minutes.
4. Meanwhile, coarsely chop or shred the chicken. Add the shredded chicken to the pot, reduce the heat to medium-low, and simmer for about 5 minutes, until heated through. Remove from the heat. Divide the soup evenly between 2 bowls.

Per Serving:

Calories: 466; Fat: 11g; Carbohydrates: 49g; Fiber: 19g; Sugar: 8g; Protein: 39g; Sodium: 1,292mg

Chicken Pasta Soup with Parmesan

Serves: 2

Prep Time: 10 minutes

Cook Time: 15 minutes

Ingredients:

- 1 tablespoon olive oil
- 1 garlic clove, minced
- 2 cups chicken broth
- 1/2 teaspoon kosher salt
- 1/4 teaspoon freshly ground black pepper
- 4 ounces ditalini pasta
- 1 cup shredded cooked chicken
- 1/2 cup grated parmesan cheese, plus additional for garnish

Directions:

1. In a stockpot or Dutch oven, heat the oil over medium-high heat. Add the garlic and cook, stirring, for about 1 minute.
2. Add the broth, salt, and pepper and bring to a boil.
3. Reduce the heat to medium, stir in the pasta, and simmer for 8 to 10 minutes, until the pasta is tender.
4. Reduce the heat to medium-low and add the chicken. Simmer until the chicken is heated through.
5. Stir in the cheese until melted and incorporated.
6. Serve hot, with extra cheese sprinkled on top.

Per Serving:

Calories: 493; Total Fat: 31g; Saturated Fat: 6g; Cholesterol: 99mg; Sodium: 729mg; Total Carbohydrates: 44g; Sugars: 2g; Protein: 41g

White Chicken Chili

Serves: 2

Prep Time: 5 minutes

Cook Time: 10 minutes

Ingredients:

- 2 cups chicken broth
- 2 cups salsa Verde
- 1 (15-ounce) can white beans, drained and rinsed
- 1 cup shredded cooked chicken
- 1/2 teaspoon ground cumin
- Kosher salt
- Freshly ground black pepper

Directions:

1. In a stockpot or Dutch oven, combine the broth, salsa, beans, chicken, and cumin. Season to taste with salt and pepper. Bring to a boil over medium heat.
2. Reduce the heat to low and simmer, uncovered, for about 10 minutes, until bubbling and heated through. Serve hot.

Per Serving:

Calories: 394; Total Fat: 19g; Saturated Fat: 1g; Cholesterol: 79mg; Sodium: 1,630mg; Total Carbohydrates: 46g; Sugars: 4g; Protein: 40g

Tomato-Basil Bisque

Serves: 2
Prep Time: 5 minutes
Cook Time: 15 minutes

Ingredients:

- 1 tablespoon avocado oil
- 1/2 yellow onion, diced
- 1/2 cup reduced-sodium vegetable broth
- 1 (14.5-ounce) can fire-roasted tomatoes
- 2 tablespoons tomato paste
- 1 teaspoon dried basil
- 1/2 teaspoon kosher salt
- Pinch freshly ground black pepper
- 1/2 cup full-fat plain Greek yogurt
- 2 teaspoons balsamic vinegar

Directions:

1. In a Dutch oven or soup pot, heat the oil over medium heat until it shimmers. Add the onion, and sauté for 3 minutes, until soft.
2. Stir in the broth, roasted tomatoes, tomato paste, and basil. Season with the salt and pepper, and stir just until combined. Cover, and simmer for 10 minutes. Remove from the heat.
3. Carefully transfer to a blender, and add the yogurt. Place the lid on the blender but remove the plug. Hold a clean kitchen towel over the opening on the lid, leaving a small space for steam to escape. Blend for 30 to 60 seconds, until very smooth.
4. Divide the soup evenly between 2 bowls. Drizzle each with 1 teaspoon of vinegar.

Per Serving:

Calories: 191; Fat: 11g; Carbohydrates: 17g; Fiber: 3g; Sugar: 10g; Protein: 8g; Sodium: 790mg

Curry Chicken Salad Sandwiches

Serves: 2
Prep Time: 10 minutes
Cook Time:

Ingredients:

- 10 ounces cooked chicken, diced
- 3 tablespoons mayonnaise
- 1 tablespoon curry powder
- 1 medium apple, peeled, cored, and diced
- Kosher salt
- Freshly ground black pepper
- 4 slices sandwich bread

Directions:

1. In a medium bowl, combine the chicken, mayonnaise, curry powder, and apple. Season with salt and pepper.
2. Cover and refrigerate for at least 30 minutes to let the flavors meld.
3. Spoon the mixture onto two slices of the bread. Top with the remaining slices of bread, and cut each sandwich in half diagonally. Serve immediately.

Per Serving:

Calories: 556; Total Fat: 22g; Saturated Fat: 4g; Cholesterol: 117mg; Sodium: 569mg; Total Carbohydrates: 40g; Sugars: 15g; Protein: 49g

Cauliflower Curry Soup

Serves: 2

Prep Time: 10 minutes

Cook Time: 15 minutes

Ingredients:

- 1 tablespoon avocado oil
- 1/2 cup chopped onion
- 1 medium sweet apple, peeled and diced
- 2 cups chopped fresh or frozen cauliflower
- 1 garlic clove, minced
- 2 teaspoons curry powder
- 1¼ cups reduced-sodium vegetable broth
- 1 (15.5-ounce) can cannellini beans, rinsed and drained
- 1/2 teaspoon kosher salt
- 1 teaspoon ground turmeric (optional)

Directions:

1. In a Dutch oven or soup pot, heat the oil over medium heat until it shimmers.
2. Add the onion, apple, cauliflower, and garlic, and sauté for 4 minutes, until soft.
3. Add the curry powder, and cook, stirring continuously, for 30 to 60 seconds, until fragrant.
4. Add the broth, then stir in the beans. Bring to a boil, reduce the heat to medium-low, and simmer for about 6 minutes. Add salt.
5. Stir in the turmeric (if using). Remove from the heat. Divide the soup evenly between 2 bowls.

Per Serving:

Calories: 449; Fat: 9g; Carbohydrates: 77g; Fiber: 18g; Sugar: 17g; Protein: 20g; Sodium: 1,741mg

Chapter 3: Salads

Avocado-Kale Salad with Seared Salmon

Serves: 2

Prep Time: 10 minutes

Cook Time: 5 minutes

Ingredients:

- 2 (4-ounce) skin-on salmon fillets
- Kosher salt
- Freshly ground black pepper
- 1 tablespoon avocado oil
- 4 cups packed chopped kale leaves, stemmed
- 1/2 Hass avocado, pitted, peeled, and sliced
- 1/4 cup chopped walnuts
- 2 tablespoons balsamic vinegar

Directions:

1. Heat a dry skillet over medium-high heat.
2. Using paper towels, pat dry the salmon fillets. Season the flesh side with salt and pepper.
3. Put the oil in the pan, and heat until it shimmers. Place the fillets, flesh-side down, and sear for 3 minutes, untouched, until they release easily from the skillet. Using a spatula, carefully flip, and cook for another 1 to 2 minutes, just until the fish flakes easily with a fork. Remove from the heat.
4. Meanwhile, in a medium bowl, combine the kale and avocado. Using your hands, gently massage the avocado into the kale for several minutes, until the kale is completely coated and feels more tender.
5. Divide the avocado-kale mixture evenly between 2 plates. Sprinkle each with 2 tablespoons of chopped walnuts. Top each with a salmon fillet. Drizzle each with 1 tablespoon of vinegar

Per Serving:

Calories: 393; Fat: 27g; Carbohydrates: 11g; Fiber: 5g; Sugar: 4g; Protein: 30g; Sodium: 398mg

Panzanella

Serves: 2
Prep Time: 5 minutes
Cook Time:

Ingredients:

- 2 cups cubed day-old baguette or rustic Italian bread
- 2 large ripe tomatoes, cut into 1-inch cubes
- 1 Persian cucumber, chopped
- 1/4 cup chopped fresh basil
- 1/3 cup simple vinaigrette dressing or store-bought
- Kosher salt
- Freshly ground black pepper

Directions:

1. In a medium bowl, toss together the bread, tomatoes, cucumber, and basil. Add the dressing and toss to mix well. Season with salt and pepper.
2. Refrigerate for 15 to 20 minutes to allow the dressing to soak into the bread and the flavors to meld. Serve chilled or at room temperature.

Per Serving:

Calories: 217; Total Fat: 8g; Saturated Fat: 0g; Cholesterol: 0mg; Sodium: 587mg; Total Carbohydrates: 32g; Sugars: g; Protein: 5g

Warm Quinoa Salad

Serves: 2
Prep Time: 5 minutes
Cook Time: 25 minutes

Ingredients:

- 1 cup reduced-sodium vegetable broth
- 1/2 cup quinoa, rinsed and drained
- 1 cup frozen edamame
- 1/4 cup water
- 3 cups packed spinach leaves, chopped into ribbons
- 1/4 cup fresh sweet basil (about 12 large leaves), chopped into ribbons
- 1 teaspoon extra-virgin olive oil
- 1 tablespoon plus 1 teaspoon red-wine vinegar
- 1/2 cup dried cherries (preferably unsweetened)
- 1/2 teaspoon freshly ground black pepper

Directions:

1. In a medium pot, combine the broth and quinoa. Bring to a boil over medium-high heat. Reduce the heat to medium-low, and simmer, covered, for 15 to 20 minutes, or until the quinoa is tender and has absorbed most of the liquid.
2. Meanwhile, put the edamame in a medium bowl with the water. Microwave on High for 3 minutes. Drain.
3. When the quinoa is ready, turn off the heat. Fold in the spinach. Cover, and set aside for 3 minutes, until the spinach is wilted.
4. Fold in the edamame, basil, oil, vinegar, and cherries, and stir until combined. Season with the pepper, and stir well. Divide the salad evenly between 2 plates.

Per Serving:

Calories: 372; Fat: 8g; Carbohydrates: 62g; Fiber: 8g; Sugar: 25g; Protein: 14g; Sodium: 217mg

Spanish-Style Chickpea and Olive Salad

Serves: 2
Prep Time: 5 minutes
Cook Time:

Ingredients:

- 1 (15-ounce) can chickpeas, drained and rinsed
- 2 celery stalks, chopped
- 1/4 cup chopped green olives
- 1/4 cup olive oil
- 2 tablespoons sherry vinegar
- Kosher salt
- Freshly ground black pepper
- 1/4 cup grated Manchego cheese

Directions:

1. In a large bowl, toss together the chickpeas, celery, and olives.
2. Add the oil and vinegar and toss to combine. Season with salt and pepper.
3. Top with the cheese and serve.

Per Serving:

Calories: 535; Total Fat: 38g; Saturated Fat: 8g; Cholesterol: 15mg; Sodium: 649mg; Total Carbohydrates: 40g; Sugars: 6g; Protein: 15g

Ginger Miso Chicken Salad

Serves: 2
Prep Time: 5 minutes
Cook Time:

Ingredients:

- 2 cups chopped romaine lettuce
- 1 cup shredded cooked chicken
- 1/4 cup cooked shelled edamame
- 1 medium carrot, shredded
- 1/4 cup simple vinaigrette with ginger miso (here) or store-bought

Directions:

1. In a large bowl, toss together the lettuce, chicken, edamame, and carrot. Add the dressing and toss to coat. Serve immediately.

Per Serving:

Calories: 214; Total Fat: 10g; Saturated Fat: 1g; Cholesterol: 54mg; Sodium: 92mg; Total Carbohydrates: 7g; Sugars: 2g; Protein: 23g

Watermelon and Feta Salad

Serves: 2
Prep Time: 5 minutes
Cook Time:

Ingredients:

- 2 cups cubed watermelon
- 1 cup diced cucumber
- 1/4 cup crumbled feta cheese
- 1/4 cup halved Kalamata olives
- 2 tablespoons red wine vinegar
- 2 tablespoons olive oil
- Kosher salt
- Freshly ground black pepper

Directions:

1. In a large bowl, combine the watermelon, cucumber, cheese, and olives and toss gently to combine.
2. In a small bowl, whisk together the vinegar and oil and season with a pinch each of salt and pepper.
3. Add the dressing to the salad and gently toss. Taste and season with more salt and pepper, if needed. Serve immediately.

Per Serving:

Calories: 326; Total Fat: 26g; Saturated Fat: 6g; Cholesterol: 17mg; Sodium: 1,021mg; Total Carbohydrates: 19g; Sugars: 11g; Protein: 9g

Pesto Pasta Salad

Serves: 2

Prep Time: 5 minutes

Cook Time: 10 minutes

Ingredients:

- 4 ounces fusilli or rotelle pasta
- 1 cup halved cherry tomatoes
- 1/4 cup herb pesto or store-bought
- 1 tablespoon chopped green olives
- 1 tablespoon olive oil
- 1/4 cup grated parmesan cheese
- Kosher salt
- Freshly ground black pepper

Directions:

1. Bring a pot of water to a boil and cook the pasta according to the package directions until al dente. Drain and rinse with cold water to cool quickly.
2. In a medium bowl, toss the pasta, tomatoes, pesto, olives, and oil. Add the cheese and toss to incorporate. Season with salt and pepper. Serve at room temperature.

Per Serving:

Calories: 462; Total Fat: 24g; Saturated Fat: 6g; Cholesterol: 18mg; Sodium: 469mg; Total Carbohydrates: 49g; Sugars: 6g; Protein: 16g

Strawberry, Steak, and Farro Salad

Serves: 2
Prep Time: 5 minutes
Cook Time: 25 minutes

Ingredients:

- 1/3 cup farro, rinsed and drained
- 1 cup vegetable stock
- Kosher salt
- 1 tablespoon avocado oil
- 1 (6- to 7-ounce) beef top sirloin steak
- Freshly ground black pepper
- 3 tablespoons red-wine vinegar
- 1 shallot, minced
- 1/2 cup dry red wine
- 2 cups or 16 small strawberries, hulled and sliced
- 3 cups packed spring salad mix

Directions:

1. In a small stockpot, combine the farro, vegetable stock, and a pinch of salt over medium-high heat. Bring to a boil, then reduce the heat to medium- low. Cover, and simmer for 25 minutes, until the farro is tender and has absorbed most of the liquid. Remove from the heat.
2. Meanwhile, in a cast-iron skillet, heat the oil over high heat until it shimmers.
3. Season the steak with salt and pepper. Add to the skillet, and sear for 3 minutes on each side, until the internal temperature reaches 145°F (for medium doneness). Transfer to a cutting board, and let rest.
4. Reduce the skillet heat to medium-low. To make the sauce, add the vinegar and shallot. Cook, stirring up the browned bits at the bottom of the skillet using a wooden spoon, for 2 minutes, until the shallot is soft.
5. Stir in the wine and half of the strawberries. Cook for about 5 minutes, until the liquid is reduced by half and the strawberries are soft. Remove from the heat.
6. Assemble the salad: Using a serrated knife and cutting against the grain, cut the steak into thin strips. Divide the salad mix evenly between 2 plates. Using a slotted spoon, top the greens with the farro and remaining strawberries. Arrange the sliced steak on top, then ladle on the strawberry sauce.

Per Serving:

Calories: 396; Fat: 12g; Carbohydrates: 41g; Fiber: 9g; Sugar: 11g; Protein: 23g; Sodium: 418mg

Bistro Salad

Serves: 2
Prep Time: 5 minutes
Cook Time: 10 minutes

Ingredients:

- 2 large eggs
- 2 cups mixed salad greens
- 1/4 cup simple vinaigrette dressing or store-bought
- 2 tablespoons crumbled blue cheese
- 2 bacon slices, cooked until crisp and then crumbled

Directions:

1. Fill a medium saucepan with water and bring to a boil. Gently add the eggs and reduce the heat to medium. Cook the eggs for 10 minutes, then remove the pan from the heat. Drain the eggs and immediately run cold water over them. Transfer the eggs to a bowl filled with ice water.
2. In a medium bowl, toss together the greens and dressing. Divide the greens between two individual serving bowls. Sprinkle blue cheese and bacon over the top of each dish.
3. Carefully crack and peel the eggs, and place an egg on top of each salad. Serve immediately.

Per Serving:

Calories: 245; Total Fat: 15g; Saturated Fat: 6g; Cholesterol: 213mg; Sodium: 875mg; Total Carbohydrates: 11g; Sugars: 7g; Protein: 16g

Tempeh Salad with Yogurt Basil Dressing

Serves: 2

Prep Time: 15 minutes

Cook Time: 5 minutes

Ingredients:

- Nonstick cooking spray, for coating the skillet
- 8 ounces tempeh, cut into 1/2 -inch strips
- 1/2 teaspoon avocado oil
- Kosher salt
- Freshly ground black pepper
- 1/2 cup full-fat plain Greek yogurt
- 1 garlic clove, minced
- 2 tablespoons water, plus more as needed
- 1 tablespoon freshly squeezed lemon juice
- 1 teaspoon dried basil
- 3 cups packed mixed salad greens
- 1/2 cup sliced grape tomatoes
- 1/4 cup finely diced red onion
- 1/2 cup unseasoned croutons (optional)

Directions:

1. Heat a small dry skillet over medium heat. Spray with cooking spray.
2. Brush the tempeh strips with the oil, and season with salt and pepper. Add to the skillet, and cook for 2 minutes on each side, until heated through. Remove from the heat, and set aside.
3. To make the dressing, in a small bowl, whisk together the yogurt, garlic, water, lemon juice, 2 pinches of pepper, and the basil. If you want a thinner consistency, add more water.
4. Assemble the salad: Divide the salad greens evenly between 2 plates. Top each with 1/4 cup of tomatoes, 2 tablespoons of onion, and 1/4 cup of croutons (if using). Split the tempeh evenly between the 2 plates. Drizzle with the yogurt dressing.

Per Serving:

Calories: 342; Fat: 13g; Carbohydrates: 29g; Fiber: 12g; Sugar: 6g; Protein: 30g; Sodium: 456mg

Lemony Brussels Sprout Slaw

Serves: 2
Prep Time: 5 minutes
Cook Time:

Ingredients:

- 1/4 cup olive oil
- 1½ tablespoons freshly squeezed lemon juice
- Kosher salt
- Freshly ground black pepper
- 8 ounces Brussels sprouts, shredded or thinly sliced
- 1/4 cup slivered almonds, toasted
- 1/4 cup freshly grated parmesan cheese

Directions:

5. In a medium bowl, whisk together the oil and lemon juice. Season with salt and pepper.
6. Add the Brussels sprouts and almonds and toss to coat.
7. Serve immediately, or cover and refrigerate for an hour to allow the flavors to meld and the sprouts to soften.
8. Just before serving, toss with the cheese.

Per Serving:

Calories: 381; Total Fat: 35g; Saturated Fat: 6g; Cholesterol: 10mg; Sodium: 238mg; Total Carbohydrates: 14g; Sugars: 3g; Protein: 11g

Poblano, Corn, and Shrimp Salad

Serves: 2

Prep Time: 10 minutes

Cook Time: 10 minutes

Ingredients:

- Nonstick cooking spray, for coating the skillet
- 8 ounces medium or large shrimp, peeled and deveined
- Kosher salt
- Freshly ground black pepper
- 1 teaspoon avocado oil
- 1 poblano pepper, seeded and diced
- 1/3 cup diced red onion
- 1 cup corn niblets, drained
- 3 cups packed coarsely chopped arugula
- 2 teaspoons extra-virgin olive oil

Directions:

1. Heat a medium dry skillet over medium heat. Spray with cooking spray.
2. Season the shrimp with salt and pepper. Add to the skillet, and cook for 1 minute on each side, just until the flesh is no longer pink. Using tongs, transfer to a plate.
3. In the same skillet, heat the oil over medium heat until it shimmers. Add the poblano and onion. Season with a pinch each of salt and pepper. Cook, stirring occasionally, for 6 minutes, until the vegetables have softened.
4. Stir in the corn, and cook for 1 to 2 minutes, just until warmed through. Turn off the heat, and return the shrimp to the skillet. Toss to combine.
5. Assemble the salad: Divide the arugula evenly between 2 plates. Top with the shrimp mixture. Drizzle each serving with 1 teaspoon of extra-virgin olive oil.

Per Serving:

Calories: 328; Fat: 9g; Carbohydrates: 38g; Fiber: 7g; Sugar: 16g; Protein: 29g; Sodium: 613mg

Lentil Salad with Cherry Tomatoes and Goat Cheese

Serves: 2
Prep Time: 5 minutes
Cook Time:

Ingredients:

- 3 tablespoons olive oil
- 2 tablespoons white wine vinegar
- Kosher salt
- Freshly ground black pepper
- 1 cup cooked lentils
- 1 cup halved cherry tomatoes
- 1/4 cup crumbled goat cheese
- 1 tablespoon minced fresh basil

Directions:

1. In a large bowl, whisk together the oil and vinegar. Season with salt and pepper.
2. Add the lentils and tomatoes and toss to coat.
3. Serve immediately, or cover and refrigerate for about an hour to let the flavors meld.
4. Just before serving, sprinkle the cheese and basil over the top.

Per Serving:

Calories: 355; Total Fat: 24g; Saturated Fat: 5g; Cholesterol: 10mg; Sodium: 142mg; Total Carbohydrates: 24g; Sugars: 4g; Protein: 12g

Mixed Greens with Pears and Blue Cheese

Serves: 2

Prep Time: 5 minutes

Cook Time:

Ingredients:

- 3 cups mixed greens
- 1 large pear, cored and diced
- 1/4 cup simple vinaigrette dressing or store-bought
- 1/4 cup crumbled blue cheese
- 2 tablespoons chopped spicy candied pecans

Directions:

1. In a large bowl, combine the greens and pear and toss gently.
2. Top with the dressing and toss to coat.
3. Sprinkle the cheese and pecans over the top. Serve immediately.

Per Serving:

Calories: 310; Total Fat: 23g; Saturated Fat: 5g; Cholesterol: 13mg; Sodium: 644mg; Total Carbohydrates: 21g; Sugars: 11g; Protein: 7g

Crunchy Apple and Cabbage Slaw

Serves: 2
Prep Time: 5 minutes
Cook Time:

Ingredients:

- 1/3 cup mayonnaise
- 1½ tablespoons apple cider vinegar
- 1½ tablespoons sugar
- 2 cups shredded cabbage
- 1 small apple, cored and cut into matchstick-size pieces
- Kosher salt
- Freshly ground black pepper

Directions:

1. In a medium bowl, mix together the mayonnaise, vinegar, and sugar.
2. Add the cabbage and apple and toss to coat well. Season with salt and pepper.
3. Serve immediately or refrigerate for up to 2 days.

Per Serving:

Calories: 338; Total Fat: 25g; Saturated Fat: 4g; Cholesterol: 13mg; Sodium: 317mg; Total Carbohydrates: 29g; Sugars: 23g; Protein: 1g

Chapter 4: Vegetarian

Sweet Potato and Black Bean Tacos

Serves: 2
Prep Time: 5 minutes
Cook Time: 45 minutes

Ingredients:

- 1 pound sweet potatoes, peeled and cut into 1-inch cubes
- 1 tablespoon olive oil
- Kosher salt
- Freshly ground black pepper
- 1 cup cooked or canned black beans
- 1 tablespoon chili powder or store-bought
- 4 corn tortillas
- 1 tablespoon chopped fresh cilantro

Directions:

1. Preheat the oven to 425°F. Line a baking sheet with parchment paper or aluminum foil.
2. Toss the sweet potatoes with the oil, and season generously with salt and pepper. Arrange in a single layer on the prepared baking sheet and bake for 35 to 40 minutes, tossing once or twice, until tender and beginning to brown.
3. In a small saucepan, combine the beans with the chili powder and heat over medium heat for about 4 minutes.
4. Warm the tortillas either wrapped in foil in the oven or over the flame of a gas burner.
5. Divide the tortillas between two serving plates, then divide the sweet potatoes evenly between them. Top with the beans. Garnish with the cilantro and serve immediately.

Per Serving:

Calories: 485; Total Fat: 10g; Saturated Fat: 2g; Cholesterol: 0mg; Sodium: 263mg; Total Carbohydrates: 89g; Sugars: 19g; Protein: 14g

Stir-Fried Tofu and Green Beans with Ginger

Serves: 2
Prep Time: 5 minutes
Cook Time: 20 minutes

Ingredients:

- 1/2 (17-ounce) package firm tofu, cut into 1-inch-thick slices
- 2 tablespoons vegetable oil, divided
- 1½ cups chopped green beans
- 2 tablespoons low-sodium soy sauce
- 2 teaspoons brown sugar
- 2 teaspoons grated fresh ginger

Directions:

1. Preheat the oven to 400°F.
2. Lay a clean dish towel flat on a cutting board or countertop. Arrange the sliced tofu on top in a single layer. Cover with a second clean dish towel and place a baking sheet on top. Place something heavy like a cast-iron pan or Dutch oven on top and let stand for 15 minutes to press out the excess water. Cut the pressed tofu into 1 -inch cubes.
3. In a large skillet, heat 1 tablespoon of the oil over medium-high heat. Add the tofu and cook, turning the slices occasionally, for 8 to 10 minutes, until golden brown. Transfer the tofu to a bowl or plate.
4. In the same skillet, heat the remaining 1 tablespoon oil over medium-high heat. Add the green beans and cook, stirring occasionally, for about 5 minutes, until tender.
5. Add the soy sauce, sugar, and ginger to the skillet and stir. Cook until the sauce begins to bubble and thicken, about 2 minutes more, then return the tofu to the pan.
6. Cook for about 3 minutes more, until the sauce coats the beans and tofu. Serve hot.

Per Serving:

Calories: 247; Total Fat: 19g; Saturated Fat: 4g; Cholesterol: 0mg; Sodium: 800mg; Total Carbohydrates: 12g; Sugars: 6g; Protein: 12g

Zucchini and Sun-Dried Tomato Mini Frittatas

Serves: 2

Prep Time: 10 minutes

Cook Time: 20 minutes

Ingredients:

- Nonstick cooking spray, for coating the muffin tin
- 1/2 cup grated zucchini (about half a zucchini)
- 3 large eggs
- 1/4 cup 2 percent milk 1 garlic clove, minced
- Kosher salt
- Freshly ground black pepper
- 2 tablespoons chopped sun-dried tomatoes
- 1/4 cup shredded cheddar cheese

Directions:

1. Preheat the oven to 350°F. Coat 4 cups of a standard muffin tin with cooking spray.
2. Wrap the grated zucchini in a paper towel, and gently squeeze over the sink to remove excess moisture.
3. In a medium bowl, whisk together the eggs, milk, garlic, and salt and pepper to taste for 2 minutes, until the eggs are foamy.
4. Pour 1 tablespoon of the egg mixture into each prepared muffin cup. Divide the zucchini evenly among the cups, fanning out the shreds. Top with the sun-dried tomatoes.
5. Pour in the rest of the egg mixture, filling each muffin cup to the top. Sprinkle each with about 1 tablespoon of cheese.
6. Bake for 16 to 17 minutes, or until the frittatas are firm and slightly browned.
7. Remove from the oven, and let sit for 1 minute. Using a knife or small spatula, loosen the frittatas from the sides, and lift out of the muffin cups.

Per Serving:

Calories: 201; Fat: 13g; Carbohydrates: 5g; Fiber: 1g; Sugar: 3g; Protein: 15g; Sodium: 233mg

Mushroom and Lentil Meatballs

Serves: 2

Prep Time: 10 minutes

Cook Time: 45 minutes

Ingredients:

- 1/4 cup dried brown lentils
- 4 ounces button or cremini mushrooms, sliced
- 2 small garlic cloves, minced
- 1 teaspoon Italian seasoning
- 1/2 teaspoon kosher salt
- 1/4 teaspoon freshly ground black pepper
- 2 large eggs, beaten
- 2 tablespoons olive oil

Directions:

1. Preheat the oven to 400°F. Line a baking sheet with parchment paper.
2. In a small saucepan, combine 1 cup water and the lentils and bring to a boil. Reduce the heat to low and cook for 10 minutes. Drain the lentils and let them cool for several minutes.
3. Transfer the lentils to a food processor and add the mushrooms, garlic, Italian seasoning, salt, and pepper. Pulse to finely chop the mixture, but don't puree it. Transfer the mixture to a medium bowl.
4. Stir the eggs into the lentil mixture. Form the mixture into walnut-size balls and arrange them on the prepared baking sheet about 1 inch apart.
5. Brush the "meatballs" with the oil.
6. Bake for about 35 minutes, until golden brown. Serve immediately or store in the refrigerator for up to 3 days.

Per Serving:

Calories: 370; Total Fat: 20g; Saturated Fat: 4g; Cholesterol: 188mg; Sodium: 656mg; Total Carbohydrates: 29g; Sugars: 2g; Protein: 19g

Teriyaki Tofu Stir-Fry

Serves: 2
Prep Time: 15 minutes
Cook Time: 15 minutes

Ingredients:

- 1 (7- to 8-ounce) block extra-firm tofu
- 1 tablespoon cornstarch
- 2 tablespoons avocado oil, divided
- 1 (10-ounce) bag frozen stir-fry vegetables
- 1/4 cup teriyaki sauce
- 1 (8.8-ounce) pouch microwavable brown rice

Directions:

1. Line a plate with a paper towel. Place the tofu on top, cover with another paper towel, and set a heavy plate on top. Drain for 10 minutes.
2. Cut the tofu into 1/2-inch dice, and transfer to a shallow bowl or plate. Toss with the cornstarch.
3. In a small skillet, heat 1 tablespoon of oil over medium heat until it shimmers. Add the tofu, and cook for about 2 minutes per side on at least 2 sides, until browned (wait to flip until the tofu releases easily from the skillet). Transfer to a plate.
4. If the skillet is dry, add the remaining 1 tablespoon of oil. Add the vegetables, and cook for about 3 minutes, until they have warmed up and show brown marks. Add the teriyaki sauce, and stir to combine. Turn off the heat. Return the tofu to the skillet, and toss to coat in the sauce.
5. Prepare the rice according to the package instructions.
6. Divide the rice evenly between 2 bowls. Top with the tofu stir-fry.

Per Serving:

Calories: 515; Fat: 20g; Carbohydrates: 63g; Fiber: 10g; Sugar: 10g; Protein: 19g; Sodium: 1,434mg

Pasta with Goat Cheese and Asparagus

Serves: 2
Prep Time: 5 minutes
Cook Time: 20 minutes

Ingredients:

- 1 pound asparagus, trimmed, cut on an angle into 1/8-inch-thick slices
- 1 tablespoon olive oil
- 1 teaspoon kosher salt, plus more if needed
- 1/2 teaspoon freshly ground black pepper, plus more if needed
- 8 ounces pasta
- 2 ounces goat cheese
- 1/4 cup heavy (whipping) cream
- Grated zest and juice of 1 small lemon

Directions:

1. Preheat the oven to 450°F. Line a baking sheet with parchment paper or aluminum foil.
2. Arrange the asparagus on the prepared baking sheet and toss with the oil. Season with the salt and pepper. Roast the asparagus until tender, about 10 minutes.
3. Meanwhile, bring a medium pot of salted water to a boil and cook the pasta according to the package directions until al dente. Drain, reserving 1 cup of the cooking water.
4. Return the pasta cooking pot to the stovetop over medium heat. Add the cheese and cream and cook, stirring, until the cheese melts and the sauce is incorporated. Add the lemon zest and juice, asparagus, and cooked pasta and stir until the pasta is coated. If necessary, add a bit of the pasta cooking water to thin the sauce. Taste and adjust the seasoning if necessary. Serve hot.

Per Serving:

Calories: 684; Total Fat: 26g; Saturated Fat: 12g; Cholesterol: 54mg; Sodium: 415mg; Total Carbohydrates: 91g; Sugars: 5g; Protein: 25g

Crispy Chickpeas with Spinach and Fried Eggs

Serves: 2
Prep Time: 5 minutes
Cook Time: 15 minutes

Ingredients:

- 2 tablespoons olive oil, divided
- 1 (15-ounce) can chickpeas, drained and rinsed
- 1/2 teaspoon smoked paprika
- Kosher salt
- 2 large eggs
- 2 cups fresh baby spinach
- Freshly ground black pepper
- 1/2 lemon

Directions:

1. In a medium skillet, heat 1 tablespoon of the oil over medium heat. Add the chickpeas, paprika, and a pinch of salt and stir to combine. Cook, stirring occasionally, for about 10 minutes, until the chickpeas are lightly browned.
2. Meanwhile, in another medium skillet, heat the remaining 1 tablespoon oil over medium-high heat. Crack the eggs into the pan and fry for about 5 minutes, until the whites are set but the yolks are still runny, reducing the heat as needed to prevent the bottom of the eggs from burning.
3. Add the spinach to the chickpeas and cook, stirring, until it wilts. Season with salt and pepper.
4. To serve, divide the chickpeas between two individual serving bowls. Top each dish with an egg and squeeze a bit of lemon juice over the top. Serve immediately.

Per Serving:

Calories: 406; Total Fat: 22g; Saturated Fat: 4g; Cholesterol: 186mg; Sodium: 180mg; Total Carbohydrates: 37g; Sugars: 7g; Protein: 18g

Zoodle Bowls with Cherry Tomatoes and Ricotta

Serves: 2
Prep Time: 5 minutes
Cook Time: 15 minutes

Ingredients:

- 3 teaspoons olive oil, divided, plus additional for garnish
- 1½ cups cherry tomatoes
- 1 garlic clove, minced
- 2 zucchini, spiralized
- Kosher salt
- Freshly ground black pepper
- 1/2 cup whole-milk ricotta cheese

Directions:

1. In a skillet, heat 1½ teaspoons of the oil over medium heat. Add the tomatoes and cook, stirring occasionally, until the tomatoes soften and begin to burst, about 10 minutes. Stir in the garlic and cook for about 30 seconds more. Transfer the tomatoes to a bowl and wipe out the pan.
2. In the same skillet, heat the remaining 1½ teaspoons oil. Add the zucchini and season with salt and pepper. Cook, tossing occasionally, for 5 to 7 minutes, until the zucchini is tender.
3. To serve, divide the zucchini between two individual serving bowls. Top each with half the tomatoes and half the ricotta. Garnish with a drizzle of oil, a pinch of salt, and a bit of pepper.

Per Serving:

Calories: 172; Total Fat: 12g; Saturated Fat: 4g; Cholesterol: 16mg; Sodium: 130mg; Total Carbohydrates: 13g; Sugars: 7g; Protein: 7g

Sweet Potato Hash

Serves: 2
Prep Time: 10 minutes
Cook Time: 20 minutes

Ingredients:

- 2 medium sweet potatoes, peeled and diced (about 2 cups)
- 1 teaspoon extra-virgin olive oil
- 1/8 teaspoon kosher salt
- 1/8 teaspoon freshly ground black pepper
- 1/2 cup frozen edamame
- 2 small or medium red bell peppers, seeded and chopped
- 1 cup quartered mushrooms
- 2 tablespoons hoisin sauce
- 1 tablespoon toasted sesame seeds (optional)

Directions:

1. Preheat the oven to 450°F. Line a baking sheet with parchment paper.
2. In a large bowl, combine the sweet potatoes, oil, salt, and black pepper. Toss until well coated. Arrange in an even layer on half of the prepared baking sheet. Bake for 15 minutes.
3. Meanwhile, in a medium bowl, combine the edamame, bell peppers, mushrooms, and hoisin sauce. Toss well.
4. Remove the baking sheet from the oven. Spread the edamame mixture on the other side of the baking sheet. Return to the oven, and bake for another 5 minutes, until the vegetables have softened. Remove from the oven.
5. Divide the vegetables evenly between 2 bowls. Sprinkle with the sesame seeds (if using).

Per Serving:

Calories: 259; Fat: 7g; Carbohydrates: 43g; Fiber: 8g; Sugar: 15g; Protein: 9g; Sodium: 484mg

Black Bean-Stuffed Bell Peppers with Plantains

Serves: 1
Prep Time: 15 minutes
Cook Time: 30 minutes

Ingredients:

- 1 (14.5-ounce) can black beans, rinsed and drained
- 1/2 cup store-bought salsa verde
- 2 large green or red bell peppers, halved lengthwise and seeded
- 1 large very ripe plantain
- 1 teaspoon avocado oil

Directions:

1. Preheat the oven to 375°F Line a baking sheet with parchment paper.
2. In a medium bowl, mix together the beans and salsa verde. Stuff each bell pepper half with one-quarter of the bean mixture. Place the stuffed bell peppers on one side of the prepared baking sheet.
3. Slice through the plantain peel lengthwise, from top to bottom, then remove. Using a sharp knife, slice the plantain on an angle to make 1/4-inch- thick rounds. Arrange the slices in a single layer on the other side of the baking sheet. Drizzle with the oil.
4. Bake for 15 minutes, flip the plantains, and bake for another 10 to 15 minutes, until the bell peppers are cooked through and the plantains are golden. Remove from the oven.
5. Divide the stuffed bell peppers evenly between 2 plates, and serve with a side of plantains.

Per Serving:

Calories: 413; Fat: 4g; Carbohydrates: 83g; Fiber: 21g; Sugar: 25g; Protein: 16g; Sodium: 496mg

Bean Empanadas

Serves: 2
Prep Time: 10 minutes
Cook Time: 20 minutes

Ingredients:

- 1 tablespoon avocado oil
- 1 small green bell pepper, seeded and diced (about 3/4 cup)
- 1/4 cup diced onion
- 1 (14.5-ounce) can pinto beans, rinsed and drained
- 2 garlic cloves, minced
- 1/3 cup raisins
- 1/2 teaspoon ground cumin
- 2 tablespoons tomato paste
- 1/3 cup beer (like a pale ale) or no-sodium-added vegetable broth
- 1/4 teaspoon kosher salt
- 1/4 teaspoon freshly ground black pepper
- 6 (5-inch) frozen empanada discs, thawed

Directions:

1. In a medium skillet, heat the oil over medium heat until it shimmers. Add the bell pepper and onion, and sauté for 2 minutes, until the vegetables have softened.
2. Stir in the beans, garlic, raisins, cumin, tomato paste, beer, salt, and black pepper. Bring to a simmer, and cook for 3 to 4 minutes, until the beer has been reduced by half. Remove from the heat.
3. Meanwhile, preheat the oven to 450°F. Line a baking sheet with parchment paper.
4. Top each empanada disc with 1/4 cup of the filling. Fold the empanadas in half, and using a fork, press the edges together to seal.
5. Arrange the stuffed empanadas in a single layer on the prepared baking sheet. Bake for 12 to 14 minutes, or until golden brown. Remove from the oven.

Per Serving:

Calories: 668; Fat: 19g; Carbohydrates: 113g; Fiber: 14g; Sugar: 21g; Protein: 22g; Sodium: 713mg

Quick Chickpea Curry

Serves: 2

Prep Time: 10 minutes

Cook Time: 15 minutes

Ingredients:

- 1 tablespoon avocado oil
- 1 to 2 tablespoons curry paste (red, green, or yellow, as desired)
- 1/2 small yellow onion, sliced
- 1 garlic clove, chopped
- 2 cups assorted chopped vegetables, like broccoli, cauliflower, carrots, or celery
- 1 (15.5-ounce) can chickpeas, rinsed and drained
- 2/3 cup canned light coconut milk
- 1 teaspoon ground turmeric
- 1/3 cup fresh basil leaves, chopped (optional)

Directions:

1. In a medium skillet, heat the oil over medium heat until it shimmers.
2. Stir in the curry paste, and toast for 30 seconds, until fragrant. Add the onion, garlic, and vegetables, and stir until well coated. Cook, stirring occasionally, for about 8 minutes, until crisp-tender.
3. Add the chickpeas, coconut milk, and turmeric, and stir to combine. Reduce the heat to medium- low, and simmer, uncovered, for about 5 minutes, until heated through. Remove from the heat. Divide the curry evenly between 2 plates. Garnish with the basil (if using).

Per Serving:

Calories: 369; Fat: 17g; Carbohydrates: 42g; Fiber: 14g; Sugar: 4g; Protein:15 g; Sodium:829 mg

Chipotle Lentil Tacos

Serves: 2

Prep Time: 5 minutes

Cook Time: 30 minutes

Ingredients:

- 2 cups reduced-sodium vegetable broth
- 1 cup dried brown or green lentils
- 1/2 teaspoon chipotle pepper powder
- 1 teaspoon garlic powder
- 1/2 teaspoon smoked paprika
- 1/2 teaspoon kosher salt
- 4 (8- or 10 -inch) whole-wheat or corn tortillas
- 1/4 cup full-fat sour cream
- 1 cup shredded Mexican-style cheese blend
- 1 cup diced seeded tomatoes

Directions:

1. In a medium pot, combine the broth, lentils, chipotle powder, garlic powder, smoked paprika, and salt. Bring to a boil over medium-high heat.
2. Reduce the heat to medium-low, cover, and simmer for 30 minutes, until the lentils are tender and have absorbed most of the liquid. Remove from the heat.
3. Fill each tortilla with one-quarter of the lentils (about 1/2 cup), 1 tablespoon of sour cream, 1/4 cup of shredded cheese, and 1/4 cup of tomatoes. Add more toppings if desired.

Per Serving:

Calories: 881; Fat: 29g; Carbohydrates: 110g; Fiber: 20g; Sugar: 9g; Protein: 48g; Sodium: 1,482mg

Sweet Potato Noodles with Sage Brown Butter

Serves: 2
Prep Time: 5 minutes
Cook Time: 15 minutes

Ingredients:

- 3 tablespoons unsalted butter
- 1/4 cup packed fresh sage leaves
- 2 medium sweet potatoes, peeled and spiralized
- Kosher salt
- Freshly ground black pepper
- Pinch ground nutmeg
- 1/4 cup freshly grated parmesan cheese

Directions:

1. In a large skillet, melt the butter over medium heat. Continue to cook until it foams and then the foam subsides. Add the sage and cook until the butter begins to brown and the leaves start to crisp, about 5 minutes. Keep your eye on the pan because the butter can burn quickly.
2. Add the sweet potato noodles and cook, stirring frequently, for 5 to 7 minutes, until tender. Season with salt, pepper, and the nutmeg.
3. Divide the noodles between two individual serving plates, sprinkle with the cheese, and serve immediately.

Per Serving:

Calories: 310; Total Fat: 20g; Saturated Fat: 13g; Cholesterol: 56mg; Sodium: 402mg; Total Carbohydrates: 27g; Sugars: 6g; Protein: 7g

Open-Face Tempeh Melts

Serves: 2
Prep Time: 15 minutes
Cook Time: 5 minutes

Ingredients:

- 8 ounces tempeh
- 1/4 cup store-bought Italian vinaigrette
- 2 thick whole-grain bread slices, cut in half
- 1/4 cup store-bought hummus
- 1 medium tomato, sliced
- 1 cup alfalfa sprouts
- 2 provolone or sharp cheddar cheese slices, cut in half

Directions:

1. Crumble the tempeh into a medium bowl. Add the vinaigrette, and toss to coat.
2. Preheat the oven to 375°F. On a small baking sheet, arrange the bread slices in a single layer. Toast for 1 minute on each side.
3. Remove from the oven, and keep the oven on. Spread 1 tablespoon of hummus on each piece of toast. Top with the tomato slices. Spoon the tempeh out of the marinade, shaking off any excess, and spread over the tomato. Top each with the sprouts and half a cheese slice. Return to the oven. Bake for another 3 minutes, until the cheese is melted and the tempeh is warm. Remove from the oven. Serve immediately.

Per Serving:

Calories: 569; Fat: 25g; Carbohydrates: 51g; Fiber: 16g; Sugar: 9g; Protein: 39g; Sodium: 750mg

Baked Pasta with White Beans

Serves: 2

Prep Time: 10 minutes

Cook Time: 45 minutes

Ingredients:

- Olive oil or nonstick cooking spray, for preparing the pan
- 4 ounces fusilli or rotini pasta
- 2 cups marinara sauce or store-bought
- 1 cup canned white beans, drained and rinsed
- 1/2 cup whole-milk ricotta cheese
- 1/2 cup shredded mozzarella cheese

Directions:

1. Preheat the oven to 350°F. Brush or spray an 8- inch square baking dish with oil.
2. Bring a medium pot of water to a boil and cook the pasta according to the package directions until al dente. Drain.
3. In the prepared baking dish, stir together the sauce, pasta, and beans. Spread the mixture into an even layer in the baking dish.
4. Dollop the ricotta cheese on top.
5. Cover the dish with aluminum foil and bake for about 30 minutes, until the sauce is bubbling.
6. Remove the foil from the baking dish, sprinkle the mozzarella cheese over the top, and bake for 10 minutes more, until the cheese is melted and beginning to brown. Serve hot.

Per Serving:

Calories: 540; Total Fat: 13g; Saturated Fat: 7g; Cholesterol: 31mg; Sodium: 1,240mg; Total Carbohydrates: 82g; Sugars: 12g; Protein: 29g

Cheesy Polenta Bake

Serves: 2

Prep Time: 5 minutes

Cook Time: 1 hour

Ingredients:

- Olive oil or olive oil spray, for preparing the pan
- 1 cup polenta
- 1 cup half-and-half
- 2 large eggs, beaten
- 3/4 teaspoon kosher salt
- 1½ cups shredded sharp white cheddar cheese, divided

Directions:

1. Preheat the oven to 350°F. Brush or spray an 8- inch square baking dish with oil.
2. In the baking dish, combine 4 cups water, the polenta, half-and-half, eggs, and salt and stir to mix well. Bake for 50 minutes.
3. Remove the baking dish from the oven, leaving the oven on, and stir in 1 cup of the cheese. Sprinkle the remaining 1/2 cup cheese over the top.
4. Return to the oven and bake for 10 minutes more. Serve hot.

Per Serving:

Calories: 657; Total Fat: 49g; Saturated Fat: 28g; Cholesterol: 319mg; Sodium: 1,113mg; Total Carbohydrates: 23g; Sugars: 1g; Protein: 32g

Pick-Your-Flavor Bean Burger

Serves: 2
Prep Time: 10 minutes
Cook Time: 10 minutes

Ingredients:

- 1 (14.5-ounce) can black beans, rinsed and drained
- 1/4 cup plain dry bread crumbs
- 1/2 cup grated yellow onion
- 1/2 cup grated carrot (or cut into matchsticks)
- 1 teaspoon garlic powder
- 1/8 teaspoon kosher salt
- Seasoning of choice: 1 to 2 teaspoons grated lime zest, 2 teaspoons sriracha, 1 teaspoon smoked paprika, or 1 tablespoon barbecue sauce (optional)
- 1 large egg
- 1 tablespoon avocado oil
- 2 thin slices cheese of your choice (optional)
- 4 butter or green-leaf lettuce leaves

Directions:

1. Put the beans in a medium bowl. Using a potato masher, mash them until lumpy (it's okay if not all beans are fully mashed).
2. Add the bread crumbs, onion, carrot, garlic powder, salt, seasoning of choice (if using), and egg. Stir until well combined. Using your hands, divide the mixture into 4 equal portions, and form flattened patties.
3. In a medium skillet, heat the oil over medium heat until it shimmers. Add the patties, and cook for 3 to 4 minutes on each side, until browned and cooked through. Top each with 1/2 slice of cheese during the final minute of cooking (if using).
4. Remove from the heat, and let rest until slightly cooled. Place each patty in a lettuce leaf.

Per Serving:

Calories: 502; Fat: 20g; Carbohydrates: 55g; Fiber: 18g; Sugar: 5g; Protein: 26g; Sodium: 724mg

Eggplant Parmesan with Pesto

Serves: 2

Prep Time: 5 minutes

Cook Time: 20 minutes

Ingredients:

- 1 small eggplant
- 2 tablespoons olive oil
- 1/2 teaspoon kosher salt
- 1/4 cup herb pesto or store-bought
- 1/4 cup panko bread crumbs
- 1/4 cup shredded mozzarella cheese
- 2 tablespoons grated parmesan cheese

Directions:

1. Preheat the oven to 400°F. Line a rimmed baking sheet with aluminum foil or parchment paper.
2. Cut the eggplant in half lengthwise, then score the cut side of each half with a crosshatch pattern about 1/2 inch deep. Place the eggplant halves on the prepared baking sheet, cut-side up. Drizzle the oil over the eggplant and season with the salt.
3. Bake for about 30 minutes, until the eggplant is tender. Remove the pan from the oven and raise the oven temperature to 475°F.
4. Spread the pesto over the cut sides of the eggplant.
5. In a small bowl, toss together the bread crumbs, mozzarella, and Parmesan. Sprinkle the mixture over the eggplant halves.
6. Bake for about 5 minutes, until the cheese is melted, bubbling, and browned. Serve hot.

Per Serving:

Calories: 410; Total Fat: 32g; Saturated Fat: 7g; Cholesterol: 20mg; Sodium: 821mg; Total Carbohydrates: 24g; Sugars: 9g; Protein: 12g

Spiced Lentils with Acorn Squash

Serves: 2
Prep Time: 10 minutes
Cook Time: 25 minutes

Ingredients:

- 1 small acorn squash, halved and seeded
- 1¾ cups reduced-sodium vegetable broth, divided
- 1 tablespoon pure maple syrup
- 3/4 cup dried brown or green lentils
- 1/4 teaspoon ground nutmeg
- Pinch ground cardamom (optional)

Directions:

1. Preheat the oven to 425°F.
2. Using a sharp knife, cut the acorn squash into 8 wedges.
3. Pour 1/4 cup of broth into a 2-quart casserole dish or an 8 -by-8-inch pan. Place the acorn squash, skin-side down, in the dish. Drizzle with the maple syrup.
4. Bake for about 25 minutes, until the squash is tender and easily pierced with a fork. Remove from the oven.
5. Meanwhile, in a small pot, combine the lentils and remaining 1½ cups of broth, and bring to a boil over medium-high heat. Reduce the heat to medium-low, cover, and simmer for 15 minutes (check periodically, and add more broth if the lentils become dry). The lentils are cooked when they are tender and have absorbed most of the liquid. Add the nutmeg and cardamom (if using), and stir until well combined. Remove from the heat.
6. Divide the acorn squash evenly between 2 plates, and spoon the lentils over the top.

Per Serving:

Calories: 362; Fat: 1g; Carbohydrates: 79g; Fiber: 11g; Sugar: 9g; Protein: 20g; Sodium: 494mg

Chapter 5: Desserts

Lemon Butter Cakes

Serves: 2
Prep Time: 5 minutes
Cook Time: 20 minutes

Ingredients:

- Nonstick cooking spray or butter
- 1/2 cup flour
- 4 tablespoons (1/2 stick) unsalted butter, melted
- 2½ tablespoons sugar
- 1 teaspoon grated lemon zest
- 1/4 teaspoon lemon extract
- Pinch kosher salt

Directions:

1. Preheat the oven to 350°F. Spray 2(6-ounce) ramekins with cooking spray. Place the ramekins on a baking sheet.
2. In a small bowl, stir together the flour, butter, sugar, lemon zest, lemon extract, and salt to combine. Press the mixture into the prepared ramekins.
3. Bake for 18 to 20 minutes, until the cakes are golden brown around the edges but still gooey in the center.
4. Place the ramekins on a wire rack and let them cool before sliding a knife around the edges and lifting the cakes out of the ramekins. Serve warm or at room temperature.

Per Serving:

Calories: 369; Total Fat: 24g; Saturated Fat: 15g; Cholesterol: 61mg; Sodium: 242mg; Total Carbohydrates: 37g; Sugars: 13g; Protein: 4g

Blueberry Clafoutis

Serves: 2

Prep Time: 5 minutes

Cook Time: 30 minutes

Ingredients:

- Nonstick cooking spray or vegetable oil
- 1 cup fresh or frozen blueberries
- 1 large egg
- 3 tablespoons reduced-fat milk
- 3 tablespoons flour
- 2 tablespoons sugar
- Pinch kosher salt

Directions:

1. Preheat the oven to 375°F. Lightly coat 2(8-ounce) ramekins with cooking spray. Place the ramekins on a baking sheet.
2. Divide the berries evenly between the ramekins, placing them in an even layer.
3. In a medium bowl, whisk together the egg, milk, flour, sugar, and salt. Pour the mixture over the berries in the ramekins, dividing it equally.
4. Bake for 30 minutes, until the top is golden and the center is set.

Per Serving:

Calories: 177; Total Fat: 3g; Saturated Fat: 1g; Cholesterol: 94mg; Sodium: 123mg; Total Carbohydrates: 33g; Sugars: 21g; Protein: 6g

Chocolate Lava Cakes

Serves: 2
Prep Time: 5 minutes
Cook Time: 12 minutes

Ingredients:

- 3 tablespoons unsalted butter, plus additional for greasing the ramekins
- 3 tablespoons plus 2 teaspoons sugar, divided
- 3 ounces dark chocolate, finely chopped
- 1 large egg
- 1 large egg yolk
- Pinch kosher salt
- 3 tablespoons flour

Directions:

1. Preheat the oven to 400°F.
2. Grease 2 (6-ounce) ramekins with butter, then sprinkle 1 teaspoon of the sugar into each of the ramekins. Shake the ramekins to distribute the sugar.
3. In a microwave-safe bowl, microwave the chocolate and butter together in 30 - second intervals, stirring after each, until completely melted and smooth.
4. In a medium bowl, whisk together the egg, egg yolk, the remaining 3 tablespoons sugar, and the salt. Add the melted chocolate and stir to combine. Finally, add the flour and stir to incorporate.
5. Divide the batter equally between the prepared ramekins and place them on a baking sheet. Bake for 12 to 14 minutes, until the top is dry.
6. Remove the ramekins from the oven and let them cool for a couple of minutes before running a knife around the inside of the ramekins to loosen the cakes. Invert the cakes onto individual serving plates and serve.

Per Serving:

Calories: 581; Total Fat: 37g; Saturated Fat: 22g; Cholesterol: 244mg; Sodium: 240mg; Total Carbohydrates: 55g; Sugars: 40g; Protein: 7g

Raspberry Crumble

Serves: 2
Prep Time: 5 minutes
Cook Time: 30 minutes

Ingredients:

- 1/2 cup flour, divided
- 1/2 cup packed brown sugar, divided
- 1/4 cup old-fashioned rolled oats
- 4 tablespoons (1/2 stick) butter, at room
- Temperature
- 1½ cups raspberries

Directions:

1. Preheat the oven to 350°F.
2. In a medium bowl, combine 6 tablespoons of the flour, 6 tablespoons of the sugar, the oats, and the butter. Mix with your hands until crumbly.
3. In a separate medium bowl, combine the remaining 2 tablespoons flour, 2 tablespoons sugar, and the raspberries and toss to coat the berries.
4. Spoon the raspberry mixture into 2 (6-ounce) ramekins. Sprinkle the crumb mixture over the top of the berries, dividing it equally between the ramekins. top of the berries, dividing it equally between the ramekins.
5. Place the ramekins on a baking sheet and bake for 30 to 35 minutes, until the tops are golden brown and the raspberries are bubbling and syrupy. Serve warm.

Per Serving:

Calories: 540; Total Fat: 25g; Saturated Fat: 15g; Cholesterol: 61mg; Sodium: 176mg; Total Carbohydrates: 77g; Sugars: 40g; Protein: 6g

Chocolate Peanut Butter Crunch Cups

Serves:
Prep Time: 10 minutes
Cook Time: 2 minutes

Ingredients:

- Nonstick cooking spray
- 2 ounces dark chocolate, finely chopped
- 1/2 teaspoon vegetable oil
- 3 tablespoons peanut butter
- 1½ tablespoons powdered sugar
- 2 tablespoons crispy rice cereal

Directions:

1. Line 4 mini-muffin cups with paper liners and coat the liners with cooking spray.
2. In a microwave-safe bowl, combine the chocolate and oil and microwave on high in 30-second intervals, stirring after each, until the chocolate is completely melted.
3. Place about 2 teaspoons of the chocolate mixture into the bottom of each cup, and tap the pan on the countertop a few times so that the chocolate spreads out and settles into the bottoms of the cups. Freeze for 10 minutes.
4. In a microwave-safe bowl, mix together the peanut butter and powdered sugar. Microwave for 20 to 30 seconds, until well combined and pourable. Spoon the peanut butter mixture into the cups on top of the first layer of chocolate, smoothing it into an even layer. Freeze for another 10 minutes.
5. Heat the remaining chocolate in the microwave in 30-second intervals, stirring after each, until it is melted again. Stir in the rice cereal, then spoon the mixture on top of the peanut butter, smoothing it into an even layer.
6. Freeze again for 10 minutes. Serve frozen.

Per Serving:

Calories: 168; Total Fat: 12g; Saturated Fat: 4g; Cholesterol: 0mg; Sodium: 55mg; Total Carbohydrates: 13g; Sugars: 10g; Protein: 4g

S'mores Cookie Cups

Serves: 2
Prep Time: 10 minutes
Cook Time: 20 minutes

Ingredients:

- Nonstick cooking spray or butter
- 3½ graham crackers (whole sheets)
- 2 tablespoons unsalted butter, melted
- 1 (1.55-ounce) bar milk chocolate (or dark chocolate), broken into several pieces
- 1/2 cup mini marshmallows
- 1/3 cup sweetened condensed milk

Directions:

1. Preheat the oven to 350°F. Lightly coat 2 (6-ounce) ramekins or muffin cups with cooking spray. If using ramekins, place them on a baking sheet.
2. In a food processor, pulse the graham crackers until they form coarse crumbs. Add the melted butter and pulse until the crumbs are fully moistened.
3. Divide the crumbs equally between the ramekins and press them down into an even layer.
4. Arrange the chocolate on top of the crumb layer, dividing it equally between the ramekins.
5. Top each with half the marshmallows, then pour half the sweetened condensed milk over the top.
6. Bake for about 20 minutes, until bubbling and golden brown on top.
7. Let cool before sliding a knife around the edges of each ramekin and lifting the cookie out of the cup. Serve warm or at room temperature.

Per Serving:

Calories: 508; Total Fat: 25g; Saturated Fat: 14g; Cholesterol: 53mg; Sodium: 324mg; Total Carbohydrates: 65g; Sugars: 51g; Protein: 8g

No-Bake Ginger-Lemon Tartlets

Serves: 2

Prep Time: 10 minutes

Cook Time:

Ingredients:

- 1/2 cup gingersnap crumbs
- 1 tablespoon unsalted butter, melted
- 1/4 cup sour cream
- 1/4 cup lemon curd
- 1/4 cup sweetened whipped cream

Directions:

1. In a small bowl, mix together the cookie crumbs and melted butter. Press the crumb mixture into the bottom and up the sides of 2 (6-ounce) ramekins.
2. In another small bowl, whisk the sour cream until it fluffs up. Add the lemon curd and whisk to incorporate.
3. Spoon the sour cream mixture into the prepared crusts. Cover the tartlets and chill for at least 4 hours.
4. Serve chilled, topped with the whipped cream.

Per Serving:

Calories: 380; Total Fat: 29g; Saturated Fat: 16g; Cholesterol: 137mg; Sodium: 355mg; Total Carbohydrates: 32g; Sugars: 15g; Protein: 5g

Chocolate Mousse

Serves: 2
Prep Time: 10 minutes
Cook Time: 2 minutes

Ingredients:

- 1/4 cup cold heavy (whipping) cream
- 2 large eggs, separated
- 2 tablespoons brewed coffee, at room temperature
- 1½ tablespoons sugar, divided
- Pinch kosher salt
- 3 ounces dark chocolate, finely chopped

Directions:

1. In a small bowl, beat the cream until it holds stiff peaks. Cover with plastic wrap and refrigerate.
2. In the top of a double boiler over simmering water, whisk the egg yolks, coffee, 1 tablespoon of the sugar, and the salt for 1 to 2 minutes, until the mixture doubles in volume and is hot to the touch.
3. Remove the bowl or pot from the heat and whisk in the chocolate until it is completely melted and the mixture is smooth. Cool to room temperature.
4. In a separate medium bowl, beat the egg whites until they are foamy, then, with the mixer running, add the remaining 1/2 tablespoon sugar and beat until the mixture holds stiff peaks.
5. Gently fold the beaten egg whites into the chocolate mixture, then fold in the chilled whipped cream until just blended. Spoon the mixture into 2 (6-ounce) ramekins. Chill in the refrigerator for at least 2 hours. Serve chilled.

Per Serving:

Calories: 450; Total Fat: 31g; Saturated Fat: 17g; Cholesterol: 227mg; Sodium: 159mg; Total Carbohydrates: 35g; Sugars: 28g; Protein: 8g

Cinnamon Bread Pudding

Serves: 2

Prep Time: 5 minutes

Cook Time: 25 minutes

Ingredients:

- Nonstick cooking spray or vegetable oil
- 1/4 cup plus 2 tablespoons reduced-fat milk
- 2 large eggs
- 2 tablespoons sugar
- 3 cinnamon bread slices (preferably slightly stale), cut into cubes
- 1/4 cup whipped cream

Directions:

1. Preheat the oven to 350°F. Grease 2(8-ounce) ramekins with cooking spray.
2. In a medium bowl, whisk together the milk, eggs, and sugar. Add the bread cubes and toss to coat the bread well.
3. Spoon the mixture into the prepared ramekins, dividing it equally. Place the ramekins on a baking sheet.
4. Bake for 25 minutes, until the pudding puffs up and is set.
5. Serve hot, topped with the whipped cream.

Per Serving:

Calories: 347; Total Fat: 13g; Saturated Fat: 6g; Cholesterol: 205mg; Sodium: 290mg; Total Carbohydrates: 42g; Sugars: 22g; Protein: 13g

Vanilla Flan

Serves: 2
Prep Time: 15 minutes
Cook Time: 30 minutes

Ingredients:

- 1/4 cup plus 1 tablespoon sugar, divided
- 1/4 cup heavy (whipping) cream
- 1/4 cup reduced-fat milk
- 2 large egg yolks
- 1/4 teaspoon vanilla extract

Directions:

1. Preheat the oven to 350°F.
2. In a small saucepan, heat 1/4 cup of the sugar over low heat until it is fully melted and golden brown. Pour it into 2(6-ounce) ramekins. Tip the ramekins to coat the bottoms completely with the syrup.
3. In a small bowl, beat the remaining 1 tablespoon sugar with the cream, milk, egg yolks, and vanilla.
4. Transfer the cream mixture to the ramekins. Place the ramekins in a baking dish, then fill the baking dish with 1 inch of boiling water. Place in the oven and bake for 30 to 35 minutes, until set.
5. Let cool to room temperature, then chill in the refrigerator overnight.
6. To serve, let the custards come to room temperature, then slide a knife around the edge of the custard and invert it onto a serving plate. The syrup will run down the sides of the flan, creating a sauce. Serve immediately.

Per Serving:

Calories: 283; Total Fat: 16g; Saturated Fat: 9g; Cholesterol: 252mg; Sodium: 33mg; Total Carbohydrates: 34g; Sugars: 32g; Protein: 4g

Chapter 6: Snacks, Sides, and Staples

Chili Powder

Serves:
Prep Time: 5 minutes
Cook Time:

Ingredients:

- 1/2 cup sweet paprika
- 2 tablespoons garlic powder
- 1½ tablespoons dried oregano
- 1½ tablespoons ground cumin
- 1 teaspoon cayenne pepper

Directions:

1. In a small bowl, combine the paprika, garlic powder, oregano, cumin, and cayenne. Store in an airtight container in a cool, dark place.

Per Serving:

Calories: 34; Total Fat: 1g; Saturated Fat: 0g; Cholesterol: 0mg; Sodium: 7mg; Total Carbohydrates: 6g; Sugars: 1g; Protein: 2g

Spicy Candied Pecans

Serves: 2

Prep Time: 5 minutes

Cook Time: 10 minutes

Ingredients:

- 2 tablespoons powdered sugar
- 1/4 teaspoon ground cinnamon
- Pinch kosher salt
- Pinch cayenne pepper
- Pinch ground nutmeg
- 1/2 cup pecans

Directions:

1. Preheat the oven to 350°F. Line a baking sheet with parchment paper.
2. In a small bowl, combine the sugar, 1 teaspoon water, the cinnamon, salt, cayenne, and nutmeg and mix well.
3. Add the pecans to the bowl and stir to coat.
4. Spread the nuts on the prepared baking sheet in a single layer. Bake for about 10 minutes,
5. until the nuts are dark brown (be careful not to let them burn).
6. Remove the nuts from the pan immediately by transferring the parchment paper to a cooling rack. The sugar coating will harden as the nuts cool. Enjoy at room temperature.

Per Serving:

Calories: 288; Total Fat: 23g; Saturated Fat: 2g; Cholesterol: 0mg; Sodium: 78mg; Total Carbohydrates: 20g; Sugars: 16g; Protein: 4g

Marinara Sauce

Serves:
Prep Time: 15 minutes
Cook Time:

Ingredients:

- 1/4 cup olive oil
- 1 (28-ounce) can crushed tomatoes
- 3 garlic cloves, minced
- 1/2 teaspoon kosher salt
- 1/4 teaspoon freshly ground black pepper
- 2 tablespoons unsalted butter
- 1 tablespoon minced fresh oregano or 1 teaspoon dried
- Pinch sugar

Directions:

1. In a medium saucepan, heat the oil over medium heat.
2. Add the tomatoes, garlic, salt, and pepper and bring to a boil. Cook, stirring frequently, for about 15 minutes, until the sauce thickens.
3. Stir in the butter, oregano, and sugar and remove from the heat. Use immediately or let cool and store for later use.

Per Serving:

Calories: 246; Total Fat: 19g; Saturated Fat: 6g; Cholesterol: 15mg; Sodium: 513mg; Total Carbohydrates: 18g; Sugars: 11g; Protein: 5g

Lemony Quinoa with Turmeric

Serves: 2
Prep Time: 5 minutes
Cook Time: 15 minutes

Ingredients:

- 1/2 cup uncooked quinoa
- Kosher salt
- 2 teaspoons olive oil
- 2 teaspoons freshly squeezed lemon juice
- 1/8 teaspoon ground turmeric
- Freshly ground black pepper
- 6 cherry tomatoes, halved
- 2 tablespoons crumbled feta cheese

Directions:

1. In a small saucepan, bring 1 cup water to a boil. Add the quinoa and a pinch of salt and reduce the heat to medium-low.
2. Cook for about 15 minutes, until the quinoa is tender and the water has been absorbed. Transfer the quinoa to a bowl and let cool.
3. In a small bowl, whisk together the oil, lemon juice, turmeric, and a pinch each of salt and pepper.
4. Add the tomatoes and the dressing to the quinoa and toss to mix. Sprinkle the cheese over the top and serve.

Per Serving:

Calories: 232; Total Fat: 9g; Saturated Fat: 2g; Cholesterol: 8mg; Sodium: 188mg; Total Carbohydrates: 30g; Sugars: 2g; Protein: 8g

Roasted Brussels Sprouts with Pesto and Parmesan

Serves: 2

Prep Time: 5 minutes

Cook Time: 20 minutes

Ingredients:

- 8 ounces Brussels sprouts, trimmed and halved through the stem end
- 1 tablespoon olive oil
- 1/4 teaspoon kosher salt
- 1/4 teaspoon freshly ground black pepper
- 2 tablespoons herb pesto, homemade (here) or store-bought
- 2 tablespoons freshly grated parmesan cheese
- 2 tablespoons crushed roasted pistachios

Directions:

1. Preheat the oven to 425°F.
2. In a medium bowl, toss together the Brussels sprouts, oil, salt, and pepper.
3. On a rimmed baking sheet, spread the Brussels sprouts in a single layer, cut-side down.
4. Roast for 20 to 25 minutes, until the sprouts are browned on the bottoms.
5. Transfer to a bowl (you can use the bowl you tossed them in before roasting) and toss them with the pesto.
6. Sprinkle the cheese and pistachios over the top and serve.

Per Serving:

Calories: 241; Total Fat: 19g; Saturated Fat: 4g; Cholesterol: 3mg; Sodium: 405mg; Total Carbohydrates: 14g; Sugars: 4g; Protein: 8g

Dry-Fried Green Beans

Serves: 2

Prep Time: 5 minutes

Cook Time: 20 minutes

Ingredients:

- 3 tablespoons olive oil
- 8 ounces green beans, halved
- 1 scallion, both white and green parts, thinly sliced
- 1 small garlic clove, minced
- 1 teaspoon sugar
- 1 tablespoon soy sauce

Directions:

1. In a large skillet, warm the oil over medium- high heat until it shimmers.
2. Add the green beans and cook, stirring, for 3 to 4 minutes, until they are browned in spots.
3. Add the scallion and garlic and toss to combine. Add 1 teaspoon water and the sugar and cook until the water evaporates, about 1 minute more. Add the soy sauce and toss to coat. Serve hot.

Per Serving:

Calories: 237; Total Fat: 21g; Saturated Fat: 2g; Cholesterol: 0mg; Sodium: 421mg; Total Carbohydrates: 12g; Sugars: 4g; Protein: 3g

Roasted Red Pepper Hummus

Serves: 2
Prep Time: 5 minutes
Cook Time: 10 minutes

Ingredients:

- 1 cup canned chickpeas, drained and rinsed
- 2 tablespoons olive oil
- 2 tablespoons tahini
- 2 tablespoons chopped roasted red peppers
- 1 tablespoon freshly squeezed lemon juice
- 1 small garlic clove, minced

Directions:

1. In a mini food processor, combine the chickpeas, oil, tahini, red peppers, lemon juice, and garlic and process until smooth. Serve immediately.

Per Serving:

Calories: 359; Total Fat: 24g; Saturated Fat: 3g; Cholesterol: 0mg; Sodium: 206mg; Total Carbohydrates: 32g; Sugars: 1g; Protein: 9g

Rice Pilaf with Almonds and Raisins

Serves: 2
Prep Time: 5 minutes
Cook Time: 25 minutes

Ingredients:

- 1 tablespoon olive oil
- 2 tablespoons diced onion
- 1 cup basmati rice
- 1 tablespoon slivered almonds
- 1 tablespoon raisins
- 1⅓ cups chicken broth, vegetable broth, or water
- 1/2 teaspoon kosher salt
- Freshly ground black pepper

Directions:

1. In a medium saucepan, heat the oil over medium-high heat. Cook the onion, stirring, for about 3 minutes, until softened. Add the rice and cook, stirring, until the grains are fully coated with oil and slightly translucent.
2. Stir in the almonds and raisins.
3. Stir in the broth and bring the mixture to a boil.
4. Reduce the heat to low, cover, and simmer for 15 to 20 minutes, until the rice is tender and the liquid has been fully absorbed. Season and serve hot.

Per Serving:

Calories: 432; Total Fat: 9g; Saturated Fat: 1g; Cholesterol: 0mg; Sodium: 426mg; Total Carbohydrates: 79g; Sugars: 3g; Protein: 8g

Barbecue Sauce

Serves:
Prep Time: 5 minutes
Cook Time: 5 minutes

Ingredients:

- 3/4 cup ketchup
- 1/3 cup apple cider vinegar
- 1/4 cup packed brown sugar
- 1 teaspoon kosher salt
- 1 teaspoon freshly ground black pepper
- 1/2 teaspoon cayenne pepper
- 1/4 teaspoon ground cinnamon

Directions:

1. In a small saucepan, stir together the ketchup, vinegar, sugar, salt, pepper, cayenne, and cinnamon, and bring to a simmer over medium heat. Cook, stirring frequently, for 5 minutes, until the sauce thickens slightly. Use immediately or cool to room temperature and store for later use.

Per Serving:

Calories: 68; Total Fat: 0g; Saturated Fat: 0g; Cholesterol: 0mg; Sodium: 547mg; Total Carbohydrates: 17g; Sugars: 15g; Protein: 1g

Simple Vinaigrette Dressing

Serves:
Prep Time: 5 minutes
Cook Time:

Ingredients:

- 1/3 cup vinegar (wine, balsamic, or apple cider)
- 1 tablespoon fresh herbs (basil, oregano, thyme, cilantro, or parsley), or 1 teaspoon dried
- 1 to 2 garlic cloves, minced
- 1½ teaspoons kosher salt
- 1 teaspoon Dijon mustard
- 1/2 teaspoon freshly ground black pepper
- 1/2 cup olive oil

Directions:

1. In a small bowl, whisk together the vinegar, herbs, garlic, salt, mustard, and pepper.
2. While whisking, slowly add the oil in a thin stream. Continue whisking until the mixture emulsifies.

Per Serving:

Calories: 149; Total Fat: 17g; Saturated Fat: 2g; Cholesterol: 0mg; Sodium: 492mg; Total Carbohydrates: 1g; Sugars: 0g; Protein: 0g

Conclusion

Love to cook but don't love the leftovers? Want to Eat healthy but don't have much time? Whether you're a newlywed or moving out on your own for the first time; looking forward to Low-Carb Diet. Low-Carb Diet Cookbook for Two helps you whip up mouthwatering meals in just the right quantities. 365-Day Perfectly Portioned Recipes in this sensational collection are just right for two diners. Best of all, each recipe includes a complete set of Nutrition Facts and more, Low-Carb Diet Cookbook for Two is your guide to quick-and-easy dishes sized right for a pair.

Sharing a meal is something most couples love to do. This cookbook takes it easy and fun to prepare dinner together. Here is that book. From simple meals to celebratory dinners, comfort food to healthy but hearty options, Low-Carb Diet Cookbook for Two.

So, what are you waiting for, act right now!

CPSIA information can be obtained
at www.ICGtesting.com
Printed in the USA
LVHW052024270821
696291LV00008B/842